PETER PAUPER PRESS
Fine Books and Gifts Since 1928

Our Company

In 1928, at the age of twenty-two, Peter Beilenson began printing books on a small press in the basement of his parents' home in Larchmont, New York. Peter—and later, his wife, Edna—sought to create fine books that sold at "prices even a pauper could afford."

Today, still family owned and operated, Peter Pauper Press continues to honor our founders' legacy of quality, value, and fun for big kids and small kids alike.

Originally published in France as *Cherche et trouve: De ville en ville*, French edition ISBN 9782215157090, © Fleurus Editions, Paris – 2016

Library of Congress Cataloging-in-Publication information available

English translation by Vesna Neskow.

First published in English in 2017 by Peter Pauper Press, Inc.
English edition copyright © 2017
Peter Pauper Press, Inc.
Manufactured for Peter Pauper Press, Inc.
202 Mamaroneck Avenue
White Plains, NY 10601 USA
All rights reserved
ISBN 978-1-4413-2475-7
Printed in China

Published in the United Kingdom and Europe by
Peter Pauper Press, Inc. c/o White Pebble International
Unit 2, Plot 11 Terminus Road
Chichester, West Sussex PO19 8TX, UK

7 6 5 4 3 2 1
Visit us at www.peterpauper.com

JULIETTE SAUMANDE

SEEK and FIND

ÉMILIE PLATEAU

AROUND THE WORLD

PETER PAUPER PRESS, INC.
White Plains, New York

Small, large, or downright gigantic. Ultramodern or with a rich thousand-year-old past. Covered with buildings and concrete or blossoming with nature. Luxurious, poor, tranquil, exuberant, sporty, artistic . . . the cities of the world have many faces!

How were they created? Who lives in them today? What are their hidden treasures? How do people celebrate there? How do they get around? And what do they eat?

NORTH AMERICA

United States
New York •
p. 25

ATLANTIC OCEAN

This amazing tour around the world will take you to 11 of our planet's most vibrant cities.

Grab your compass, your binoculars, and your map. Let's get going!

Brazil
Rio de Janeiro
p. 13 •

SOUTH AMERICA

WHAT AN ADVENTURE!

Wonderful things are hidden in each city you will visit: objects, monuments, animals, people, and more. It's up to you to find them!

Take a look at this traveler: he plays hide-and-seek in every city. Will you be able to spot him?

Russia

• Moscow
p. 15

EUROPE

Paris
p. 5
France

Venice
p. 19

Italy

ASIA

Beijing •
p. 11

China

Cairo
p. 7

Egypt

Dubai •
p. 17

**United Arab
Emirates**

Jaipur
p. 23

India

**PACIFIC
OCEAN**

AFRICA

Kenya

• Nairobi
p. 21

OCEANIA

**INDIAN
OCEAN**

Australia

Sydney •
p. 9

4

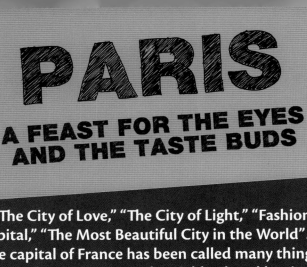

PARIS
A FEAST FOR THE EYES AND THE TASTE BUDS

"The City of Love," "The City of Light," "Fashion Capital," "The Most Beautiful City in the World"... the capital of France has been called many things over the centuries. Each neighborhood has its unique identity, from the cool Marais, with its pre-revolutionary buildings, to the fancy 16th Arrondissement with its museums. Not to mention the Latin Quarter full of students, working-class Place Clichy, or the Triangle de Choisy, one of Paris's Asian neighborhoods. This is a vibrant and bustling city.

A RECORD-BREAKING SYMBOL

Built for the Universal Exposition of 1889, the Eiffel Tower was not meant to last! But to avoid wasting two years of construction, 18,038 pieces of iron, and 2.5 million rivets, its creator, Gustave Eiffel, had a weather station and a telegraph relay installed in the tower. Later, the tower's antennae—some of them placed 1,063 feet high—were used for radio and television broadcasts.

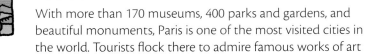

TOURIST DREAM CITY

With more than 170 museums, 400 parks and gardens, and beautiful monuments, Paris is one of the most visited cities in the world. Tourists flock there to admire famous works of art like the *Mona Lisa*, a portrait by Leonardo da Vinci housed in the Louvre Museum. You can also find unusual museums in the French capital, such as the Museum of Magic, the Museum of Perfume, or the Fan Museum.

TO THE BASTILLE!

The history of Paris is filled with wars, revolutions, attacks, and protests of all sorts. Paris is where the French Revolution began, with the storming of the Bastille prison on July 14, 1789. Today, the only thing left of this prison is its outline, marked on the ground by cobblestones.

MORE THAN A CENTURY OF THE METRO

With 16 lines, 303 stations, and 127 miles of tracks, Paris's Metro (the metropolitan public transit system) carries more than 5 million travelers a day. Its Art Nouveau entrances, created by the architect Hector Guimard, date from the opening of the first Metro line in 1900. The Metro is also home to 16 "phantom" empty stations: stations that have been closed, moved, or never even opened!

BONES BENEATH THE SIDEWALKS

In the 1780s the Holy Innocents' Cemetery was overflowing! So Paris decided to dig up the bones and throw them into the ancient tunnels south of the city. The bones of about 6 million Parisians were piled in the tunnels, or *catacombs*. Soon, this spooky jumble was organized with altars and plaques. Visitors can even walk through over a mile of underground tunnels lined with skeletons!

GOURMET MEALS

France is famous around the world for its food, and Paris has its own tasty specialties. You can try them in the city's fancy restaurants, but also at the corner bakery or bistro. On the menu: croque-monsieur (ham and grilled cheese sandwich), onion soup, mille-feuille (layered pastry and cream), chocolate éclair, financier (almond cake) . . .

FIND THEM ALL!

CAIRO

HISTORY ON EVERY STREET CORNER

Built on the banks of the Nile and sitting at the doorstep of the desert, Cairo is the capital of Egypt and one of the largest cities in Africa. 7.8 million people live here! In Cairo, the historic Muslim neighborhood abuts the old Christian city, remains of ancient buildings surround skyscrapers, and working-class towns look out on the great pyramids. This is a veritable labyrinth, teeming with pedestrians, vendors, and tourists.

THE GIFT OF THE NILE

Egypt has had this nickname for thousands of years. Why? The mighty Nile river allowed ancient Egyptians to build an amazing civilization despite the harsh climate of their country, which is 90% desert. Farmers can find everything they need near the banks of the Nile, and today it is still home to many animals and plants, such as water buffalo, papyrus, and flax.

JOURNEY THROUGH TIME

In ancient Egypt the region's great city was not Cairo but nearby Memphis. Nevertheless, today people can glimpse the time of the pharaohs at the Egyptian Museum, which houses 160,000 objects. Thousands of these belong to the famous treasure of Tutankhamun. And of course, the Sphinx and the three great pyramids of Giza are not far away!

THE KHAN EL-KHALILI SOUQ

The biggest and most famous souq (marketplace) of Cairo is situated in the heart of the Islamic quarter. Travelers shop for all sorts of wares there: from gold objects to aromatic spices, from models of pyramids to dance costumes. Nearby is Café el-Fishawy, where people have been enjoying hibiscus infusions and mint tea since 1773.

THE SALADIN CITADEL

Built in the Middle Ages by the great Sultan Saladin, the citadel defended Cairo for many centuries. Each new ruler of Egypt lived there and added his personal touch: a wall, a tower, a palace, or a mosque, like the superb Mosque of Muhammad Ali whose grand silhouette adds elegance to the city skyline. Today there are also a number of museums in the Saladin Citadel.

THE OLD CITY

The oldest neighborhood of the city was built in the ancient fortress of Babylon, constructed by the Romans. It shelters Coptic churches—that is, Egyptian Christian churches, and particularly the famous "hanging church" El Muallaqa. Though more plain on the outside, inside these churches are filled with magnificent paintings, sculpted wooden doors, and marble columns.

THE "CITY OF THE DEAD"

Cairo is crowded and housing can be difficult to find, but people have gotten creative in making homes for themselves. At el-Arafa they have settled in a giant cemetery. The tombs, which look like small houses, have been equipped with running water and electricity. More than 500,000 people live there today!

SYDNEY
NATURE IN THE CITY

Deserts, droughts, sandstorms, tornadoes . . . Australian nature can be hostile. But in the large cities of the Pacific coast nature becomes a refuge. Amid the bustle of Sydney, people enjoy the seashore, the large green spaces, and the animals that live there. Sydneyites love being outdoors, whether they're playing sports, fishing, or enjoying a barbecue!

SYDNEY BEFORE SYDNEY

The first inhabitants of Sydney, the Aborigines, arrived there about 50,000 years ago. They belong to the oldest living civilization in the world. Today, visitors can learn about their traditions in the markets, such as the Blak Markets of Bare Island, or their history at the Australian Museum.

SHIPPING OUT PRISONERS

The explorer James Cook did not "discover" the Sydney area until 1770, and then he claimed it as British territory (even though it was already home to Aborigines). Starting in 1788, Great Britain began sending its first colonists . . . prisoners shipped to Australia as punishment! British colonists struggled with isolation, hunger, and disease. Things were even harder for the Aborigines whose home the new colonists were occupying.

IN THE WATER!

Sydney is one of the largest natural ports in the world. Ferries, water taxis, kayaks, and yachts constantly crisscross the water on their way to the many islands dotting the seas. Or they compete in the great Sydney-Hobart yacht race. The port is also the best place for whale watching during the humpback whale migrations from May to November.

THE SYDNEY OPERA

Sails? Shells? Whatever its structures represent, the opera house is definitely the symbol of the city. Built in 1973, it was designed by the Danish architect Jørn Utzon, who wanted to make "the building into a living thing." More than 1,500 shows are staged at the Sydney Opera each year.

AN INCREDIBLE MENAGERIE

Taronga Zoo houses more than 4,000 animals of 350 different species, including many native to Australia and the neighboring islands: koalas, kangaroos, bilbies, Tasmanian devils, tree-kangaroos, wombats, and more. The Sky Safari, a cable car, even lets you look at the animals from very high up. Useful if you don't want to rub elbows with crocodiles and lions!

BONDI BEACH

The most famous beach in Australia is just a few miles from the center of Sydney. It's a paradise for surfers, swimmers, and travelers who come from around the world to enjoy the fine sand and rolling waves. Some compete in sea rescue competitions, or enjoy the Christmas celebrations in the middle of the Australian summer.

BEIJING
AGELESS POWER

Beijing offers glimpses into millennia of history: from the era of prehistoric "Peking Man," to the times of the Mongol invader Genghis Khan, to the period of Chairman Mao Tse-tung. It is also an ultramodern city, with advantages and drawbacks: pollution and endless traffic, but also many green spaces that allow citizens moments of peace and spirituality.

THE FORBIDDEN CITY

The construction of the 980 buildings of the Imperial City, which was the center of power for five centuries, required the continuous labor of a million workers for 14 years. Whoever entered the city without permission was executed—hence the nickname "Forbidden City." Today it is a fabulous museum that houses the treasures of more than 20 emperors.

TIANANMEN SQUARE

The Square of "the Door to Celestial Peace" is among the largest squares in the world, and the setting for major moments in Chinese history. Here, Chairman Mao Tse-tung proclaimed the creation of the Peoples' Republic of China in 1949, massive military parades took place, and great political demonstrations occurred.

SYMBOLS EVERYWHERE

Beijing is home to many temples (Buddhist, Taoist, and Confucian) with symbolic architecture. The "Hall of Prayer for Good Harvests" is round (representing heaven), on a square foundation (symbolizing the earth), and decorated with four large inside columns (the seasons) and 24 smaller outside columns (12 months and 12 hours).

CUTTING-EDGE BEIJING

Beijing also has many ultramodern areas, where enormous shopping malls stand alongside skyscrapers. The city's fantastic architecture demonstrates China's inventiveness. The National Stadium, nicknamed "The Bird's Nest," is one of the largest steel structures on the planet. In the winter it's used for skiing!

TIME TO EAT!

Here, cooking is a national treasure. Special dishes from all over China can be found in Beijing, served in fancy restaurants or from simple street stands like the ones in Wangfujing Snack Street. On the menu: dumplings, sautéed noodles, roast duck, Mongolian hot pot, or even fried scorpion, all washed down with tea.

WALK THE HUTONGS

Hutongs are the narrow alleys that connect the large streets of the city. Bordered by traditional and contemporary houses, these historic lanes are slowly disappearing because they hold up traffic. Here you'll find mahjong players, cyclists . . . and plenty of tourists!

RIO DE JANEIRO
RHYTHM AND COLORS

Rio is nicknamed "The Marvelous City." Not surprising when you see the beautiful bay, dotted with hills and bordered by beaches. Former capital of Brazil, Rio has lost that title but is the most visited city in South America today. Descendants of indigenous peoples, settlers, slaves, and masses of travelers who came from around the world over the course of centuries, the residents of Rio ("Cariocas") are proud of their heritage.

HEAVENLY BEACHES

Miles of fine sand along a turquoise sea! The beaches of Ipanema and Copacabana are famous throughout the world. Cariocas (Rio locals) and tourists go there to tackle the waves, play beach volleyball, or enjoy açai ice cream, made from the fruit of native palm trees. On New Year's Eve, thousands of spectators dressed in white go to Copacabana for the traditional fireworks.

CLIMB IT!

Rio is hilly. Famed Sugarloaf Mountain seems to surge up out of the sea, rising 1,299 feet high. Rock climbing fans love it, but to get up there effortlessly, take the cable car. It's over 100 years old! At the peak of Mount Corcovado stands the enormous statue of Christ the Redeemer, truly the symbol of the city. It is 125 feet tall, and each hand weighs 8 tons!

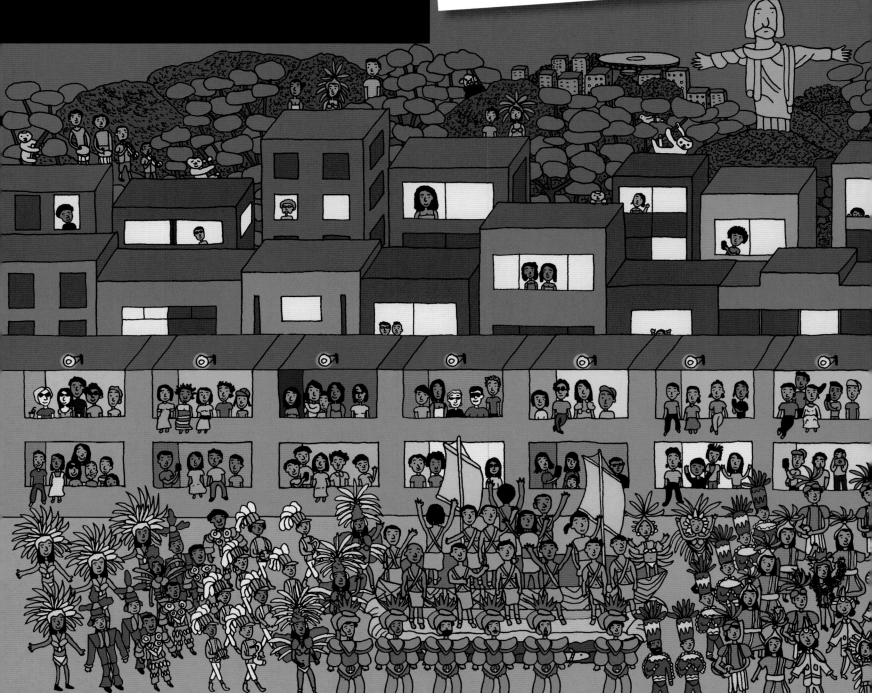

THE FAVELAS

One third of Cariocas live in "favelas," working-class neighborhoods where conditions are difficult but culture is strong. Houses may be made of reused materials, and in some places there are few schools, hospitals, and roads. Favela residents use creative ingenuity to build homes and communities. It's also in these neighborhoods that two of Brazil's most famous musical genres were invented: samba and carioca funk.

A PASSION FOR SPORTS

Maracanã Stadium, one of the world's most famous soccer (or football) fields, is located in Rio. Great games were played on its lawn, like the final match of the 2014 World Cup. And it is here that some players became legends: Pelé made his 1,000th goal in this stadium! In the summer of 2016, Rio hosted the first Olympic Games to take place in South America.

GRAND CARNIVAL

Carnival takes place in Rio every year in February. Over-the-top costumes, masquerades, concerts performed by neighborhood orchestras—it's a time to go wild! On the Sambadrome, a large boulevard specially dedicated to the Samba Parade, floats and dancers from the best samba schools file past the audience and the judges, who choose the school that will be champion for the year.

A FOREST IN THE CITY

The Tijuca Forest, located within Rio, is a tropical rainforest and one of the largest urban forests in the world. Tended since its creation in 1861 on former coffee plantations, it shelters many species of plants and animals. Some of these—such as the buffy-tufted marmoset, maned sloth, and channel-billed toucan—are threatened or endangered.

FIND THEM ALL!

14

MOSCOW

OPULENT QUEEN

Moscow: medieval, Orthodox, Soviet, punk! The capital of the Russian Federation and the former Soviet Union has a rich and eventful history, which is reflected in its impressive buildings and grand museums. Here you can visit the world's most luxurious subway stops—the stations have marble floors and columns covered in titanium and countless gold decorations. In Moscow, everything is on a grand scale. Sometimes you feel like you're in a play at the theater. Celebrations and parades are part of the city's rhythm.

THE HEART OF POWER

Red Square is one of the most famous squares in the world. It began as a place of executions, revolutions, and military parades. Many hundreds of years ago, it became the site of the Kremlin fortress, where a long line of tsars (kings), dictators, and presidents led one of the most powerful countries on the planet. The tomb of Vladimir Lenin, founder of the Soviet Union, is also located here.

ROW OF ONIONS

Saint Basil's Cathedral, a great symbol of Moscow, was built in 1560 by Tsar Ivan the Terrible to celebrate a war victory. Each of its nine chapels is topped by a dome shaped like an onion, giving this monument the look of a magical castle. Inside, the walls are covered with golden frescoes and icons, paintings of saints often seen in the Orthodox Christian religion.

IN ORBIT

The first human and animal to orbit the world in outer space were launched from the Soviet Union: Yuri Gagarin and Laïka the dog. Moscow honors them with the immense 351-foot-high Monument to the Conquerors of Space, the statues bordering the avenue Cosmonauts Alley, and the enormous Memorial Museum of Cosmonautics.

ON STAGE

The Bolshoi is one of the most famous and respected theaters in the world. Ballet, opera, plays: This is where many classics were first performed, such as Tchaikovsky's *Swan Lake*. With its 200 dancers, the Bolshoi Ballet is among the largest and most acclaimed ballet companies on this planet.

THE WORLD CAPITAL OF THE CIRCUS

In Moscow people take the circus seriously. The city's first circus, made of wood, was built in 1830. The world's first circus school was founded here in 1926. Today, the Great Moscow State Circus on Vernadskogo Avenue holds 3,300 spectators and presents shows on the floor, on ice, or on water . . . all in the same room!

GIANTS

To celebrate the 800th anniversary of the city, Soviet leader Joseph Stalin decided to build eight skyscrapers. Seven were completed. They tower 17 to 36 stories tall, embellished with spires and sculptures. These buildings (which were influenced by buildings in New York) are nicknamed "The Seven Sisters" of Moscow.

DUBAI
HEADING TO THE FUTURE

Once a modest village of Bedouins, or Arab nomadic people, Dubai is now the most important city and port of the United Arab Emirates. It is also a crossroads between cultures. With its extravagant skyscrapers and its ultramodern shopping malls, Dubai is a futuristic metropolis but retains traces of history and heritage. A city of wealth, Dubai constantly challenges and transforms itself, setting new world records as it goes.

ALWAYS MORE

Dubai's Burj Khalifa is 163 stories and 2,717 feet high. It is the highest tower in the world. Another record: the Burj al-Arab Hotel is the most luxurious hotel on the planet (seven stars!), as well as the most recognizable, because it looks like a ship's sail. Dubai also boasts underwater hotel rooms and an indoor ski resort in the middle of the desert.

ONE HUMP OR TWO?

Today's Dubai is far from the little Bedouin village it started as. But its legacy of the desert is still felt in the respect given to . . . camels. Camel races are still common (even if jockeys today are robots) and beauty contests are still held for these animals.

AS-SALAAM-ALAIKUM

The official religion of the United Arab Emirates is Islam, and in Dubai Muslim traditions are respected in grand style! The holiday Eid al-Fitr, the end of Ramadan, is celebrated with spectacular fireworks over the city. The splendid Jumeirah Mosque, built in 1976 but with the architectural style of the Middle Ages, holds 1,200 people.

IN MID-FLIGHT

Another Bedouin legacy is falconry. This sport is still practiced by rich Dubaians. They compete in the Fazza Championship for Falconry, which includes the "telwah" hunting round: falcons hunting living prey. There is even a falcon hospital, which cares for and protects these birds of prey, many species of which are endangered.

MAN-MADE ISLANDS

Dubai gets much of its wealth from tourism and goes out of its way to attract visitors. The city moved tons and tons of sand to create completely artificial archipelagos. Man-made islands form the shape of a palm tree (The Palm) and even a map of the world (The World).

SHOPPER'S PARADISE

From the traditional souk to numerous malls, shopping is practically a national sport. The Dubai Mall is one of the largest in the world: its 1,200 boutiques, 33,000-animal aquarium, Olympic ice skating rink, and waterfalls attract more than 750,000 visitors each week.

VENICE
FEET IN THE WATER

The first inhabitants of the "City of Water" fled there to escape invading armies in the early Middle Ages, and they never regretted it. On its islands, in the shelter of its lagoon, Venice turned its focus to the sea and trade. Marco Polo set out for far-away China from its port. The city is worldly in the arts as well as commerce—in 1932, the first-ever international film festival took place in Venice.

THE SERENISSIMA

Venice was an ancient independent trading power. Led by a doge (a leader first elected by the people, then later by the nobles), the "Serenissima" (Most Serene Republic of Venice) built top-quality boats and was home to talented navigators. Thanks to its seafaring power, Venice ruled the water.

A WATER LABYRINTH

The city of Venice is a group of 118 islands separated by 177 canals and connected by 455 bridges. To get around, you have to walk, since cars are forbidden, or borrow a boat. You could try a vaporetto (steam-driven boat-bus), gondola (a flat-bottomed boat steered with a single oar), or traghetto (large gondola shuttling along the famous Grand Canal).

PALACES EVERYWHERE

Venetian palaces show off the history of the city, evidence of its past wealth and power. Many stand right at the edge of the water, without a sidewalk, like those along the Grand Canal. Made of bricks, the buildings rest on countless wooden pillars and are often covered in thin façades of marble.

EVERYTHING IS ALLOWED!

The Carnival in Venice dates back to the Middle Ages. The celebration kicks off with the "flight of the angel," when a young girl hanging from a rope launches off the bell tower of Saint Mark's Square. Then strange characters in disguises and masks invade the streets and palaces. A children's carnival, a nautical parade, a costume competition, processions: it's all part of 10 days of madness and extravagance!

SO MUCH ART!

Throughout its history Venice welcomed many great artists, such as the painters Titian, Tintoretto, and Veronese; the musician Antonio Vivaldi; and the writer Carlo Goldoni. Splendid museums display this rich heritage. On the nearby islands of Murano and Burano, master glassblowers and world-renowned lacemakers practice their art.

AND YET, IT'S SINKING

Unfortunately, the future of Venice is in peril. The silt-filled canals prevent the water from flowing properly. Enormous cruise liners create waves that damage the foundations of the buildings. And global warming is causing a worldwide rise in ocean levels that threatens to submerge the city.

NAIROBI
MODERN AND INVENTIVE

The capital of Kenya is a young and dynamic city. Its name means "cool water" in the Maasai language. The city benefits from a great location: close to the equator but at an altitude of 5,577 feet, so its inhabitants enjoy a comfortable climate all year round. Nairobi is proud of the area's natural environment, and works to protect it.

THE CRADLE OF HUMANITY

The history of humanity began in the nearby savannah of the Great Rift Valley. The National Museum of Nairobi traces this long adventure, thanks to an outstanding collection of fossils found in the region, such as those of the "Turkana Boy." This specimen is one of our distant ancestors, an early *Homo erectus*, whose nearly complete skeleton is 1.5 million years old.

A BRITISH START

The city of Nairobi was founded by British colonists in 1899. At first it was a railroad depot along the tracks connecting Uganda and Kenya. Despite plague epidemics and fires, Nairobi gained importance and became the capital of British East Africa. Many Europeans went there to hunt.

A MOSAIC OF PEOPLES

Many different people live in the Nairobi area. Nairobians represent over 40 tribes, including the Maasai (nomadic livestock farmers), the Kikuyu (farmers), and the Luo (goat and cattle breeders). Today, these peoples fight for the preservation of their traditions and the recognition of their rights.

FABULOUS FABRICS

Kenyan entrepreneurs and artists have made Nairobi one of the world's great textile and fashion centers. Famous designers visit Nairobi to buy fabrics from local boutiques, many of which have been run by the same family for generations. On the city's best fabric-shopping streets, you'll find both traditional and cutting-edge designs.

FACING THE FUTURE

In 1963 Kenya gained its independence, and Nairobi became the capital of the new country. It grew fast and high. Skyscrapers more than 30 stories tall sprang up from the center of the city, and the population has surpassed 3 million. With more people than housing, "unofficial" neighborhoods have formed, the biggest of which is Kibera. Lacking many resources, Kibera is crowded and poor, but local groups work to provide schools, sanitation, and more.

WILDLIFE IN THE CITY

Nicknamed "the green city under the sun," Nairobi has many parks and golf courses. It also has an elephant orphanage and a giraffe sanctuary. Its national park is the only great animal reserve right next to a capital city. There you can find 400 species of animals, including birds, rhinoceroses, lions, and zebras.

FIND THEM ALL!

JAIPUR
THE CITY OF A THOUSAND COLORS

Chaotic, busy, punctuated by oases of calm, Jaipur has many hidden treasures. The capital of the state of Rajasthan, India attracts travelers from all over the planet. Precious gems are cut there, and the city is one of the world's largest exporters of gold and diamonds. Nicknamed "the pink city of India," Jaipur hosts a collection of dazzling palaces with finely chiseled façades and pink walls.

FIND THEM ALL!

KEEP MOVING!

There are people everywhere in Jaipur. The streets teem with pedestrians, rickshaws (tricycles that serve as taxis), cars, motorcycles, jam-packed buses, and even camels! The smallest vehicles weave in and out between larger ones, which move aggressively so as not to be overtaken. And horns honk non-stop.

THE GLORY OF THE MAHARAJAHS

The splendors left behind by Rajasthan's historic rulers still shine. Outside the city lies Amer Fort, from where they reigned for more than 140 years. Among the dozens of palaces in Jaipur stands the Hawa Mahal ("Palace of the Winds"), whose hundreds of windows allowed the women of the royal household to see the street without being seen.

HEAD IN THE STARS

The Jantar Mantar Observatory was built in the 1720s by Maharajah Jai Singh II, founder of the city. It has 17 instruments of astronomic size! They are made of stone and allow people to observe celestial happenings very precisely. The sundial, for example, tells time with two-second accuracy.

SACRED JAIPUR

Most of the inhabitants of Jaipur are Hindu, and practice in the many temples of the city. Gleaming marble, delicately sculpted statues, flamboyant frescoes: these all celebrate the gods Vishnu, Lakshmi, Ganesh, and others. Many festivals honor them, such as Teej (Monsoon Festival) and Gangaur.

ANIMALS AT EASE

Cows are sacred here. They meander along the streets at will—don't rush them! At the Galtaji temple, monkeys are kings. They won't hesitate to jump on tourists and snatch their peanuts. In March, the Elephant Festival includes a beauty pageant of pachyderms, as well as polo matches.

A BIT OF CALM

Yoga is a combination of physical exercise and meditation that originated in India thousands of years ago. It is very popular in Jaipur. Yoga teachers offer free outdoor classes in Central Park. There is even laughter yoga: You force yourself to laugh until the laughter becomes natural. A good mood and high energy are guaranteed!

NEW YORK
THE CITY THAT NEVER SLEEPS

The 5 boroughs of New York (Queens, Brooklyn, Manhattan, the Bronx, and Staten Island) are a mosaic of vastly different people who live side by side. One of the world's most powerful stock exchanges is on New York's Wall Street, and some New Yorkers live in luxury while others struggle to pay for tiny apartments. City of business, city of the arts, green city (organic farms have sprouted on some rooftops!), gateway to America, site of tragedy . . . New York forges ahead with energy and endurance.

IN THE HEART OF THE CITY

The city's most well-known skyscrapers are located on the island of Manhattan, notably the Empire State Building and the Chrysler Building. The tallest building in the country, One World Trade Center, stands on the site of the famous Twin Towers destroyed in the attack on September 11, 2001.

THE AMERICAN DREAM

Millions of people escaping war, misery, or oppression came to New York to try their luck. After crossing the Atlantic, the first thing they saw was the giant Statue of Liberty. Between 1892 and 1954 these immigrants disembarked from their ships at Ellis Island, where they were examined and questioned, then allowed (or not) to enter the United States. New York owes its unique and thriving culture to immigrants, many of whom still come to live here.

NEW YORK, NEW YORK

New York is a center for all kinds of art. Here you find world-renowned museums, such as the Guggenheim or MoMA (Museum of Modern Art); countless art galleries; and grand theaters like the ones around Broadway, the famous district. The city is also the backdrop for many movies, books, and comics. It's even the model for Gotham City, where Batman lives.

THE WORLD IN NEW YORK

Two of every five New Yorkers were born abroad, and as many as 800 languages are spoken in this diverse city. New Yorkers who came from afar (long ago or recently) sometimes gather in neighborhoods where their language and culture are practiced and honored: Chinatown, Little India, Jamaica, Koreatown, Little Senegal, Little Italy . . .

CENTRAL PARK

This is the green heart and soul of the city, where New Yorkers from all walks of life turn up. The gigantic park includes vast lawns, woods, a lake, gardens, restaurants, and even a theater and a zoo! It's the ideal spot for jogging, listening to an open-air concert, or bird watching, all in the heart of the urban bustle.

THERE'LL BE FUN AND GAMES

New York hosts many great sports events, such as the U.S. Open tennis matches at Flushing Meadows, or the New York Marathon, which has more than 45,000 runners each year! But many New Yorkers take greatest pride in the Yankees, the baseball team that played in 40 World Series and won 27, a record!

Did you find everything on the Seek and Find pages? Try this extra challenge! The following people, objects, and animals are hidden throughout the 11 cities in this book. It's up to you to track them down!